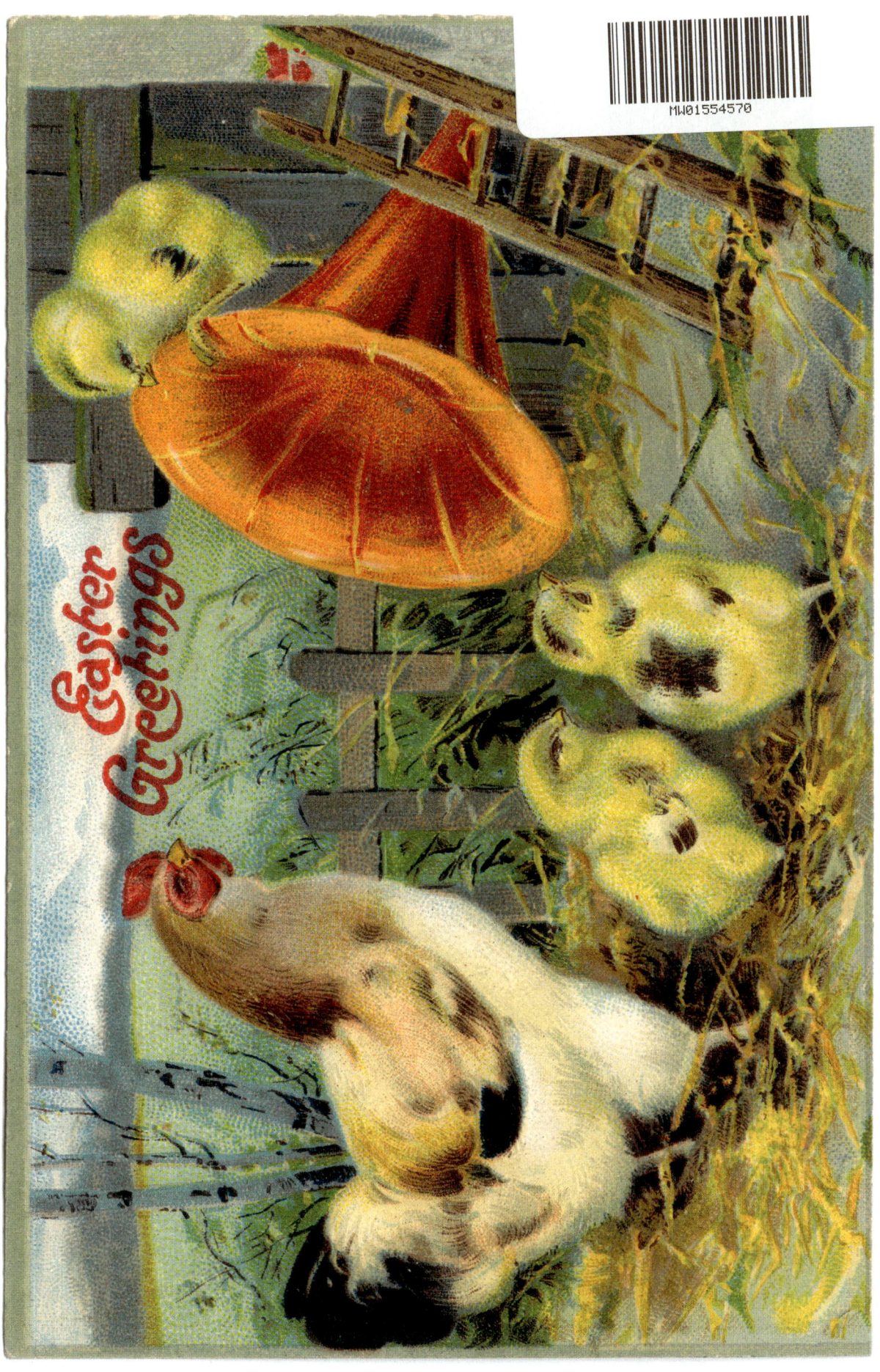

To remove pictures for framing we suggest that
you carefully cut the page out near the spine and then trim
any excess paper with blade and ruler to fit to size.

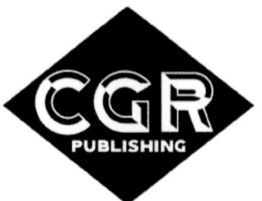

**Oversized Images of Easter Volume 1:
Premium Vintage Ephemera for Scrapbooking and Crafts**

by Kayleel Kim

Copyright © 2021 Inecom, LLC.
All Rights Reserved

More books at
CGRpublishing.com

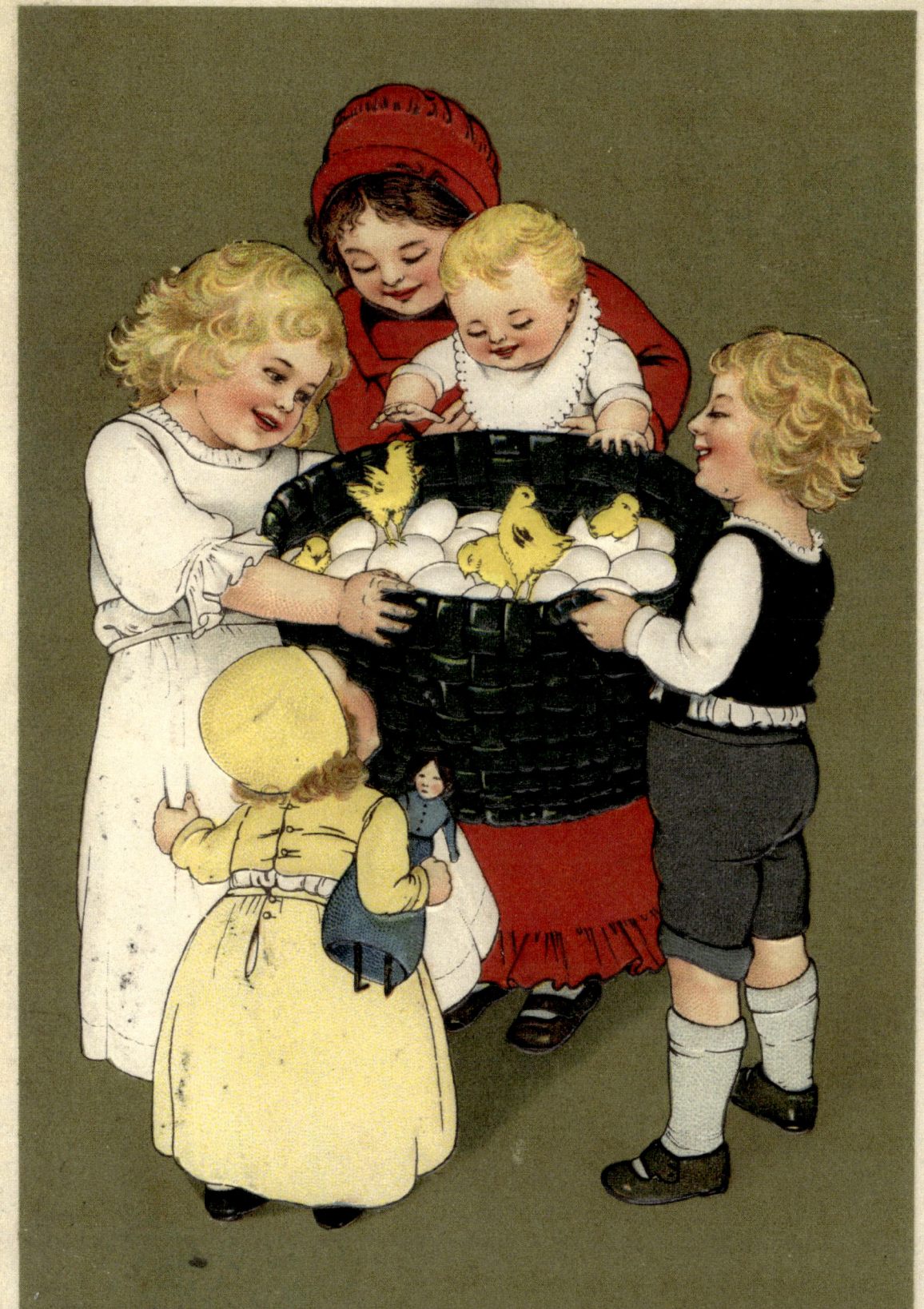

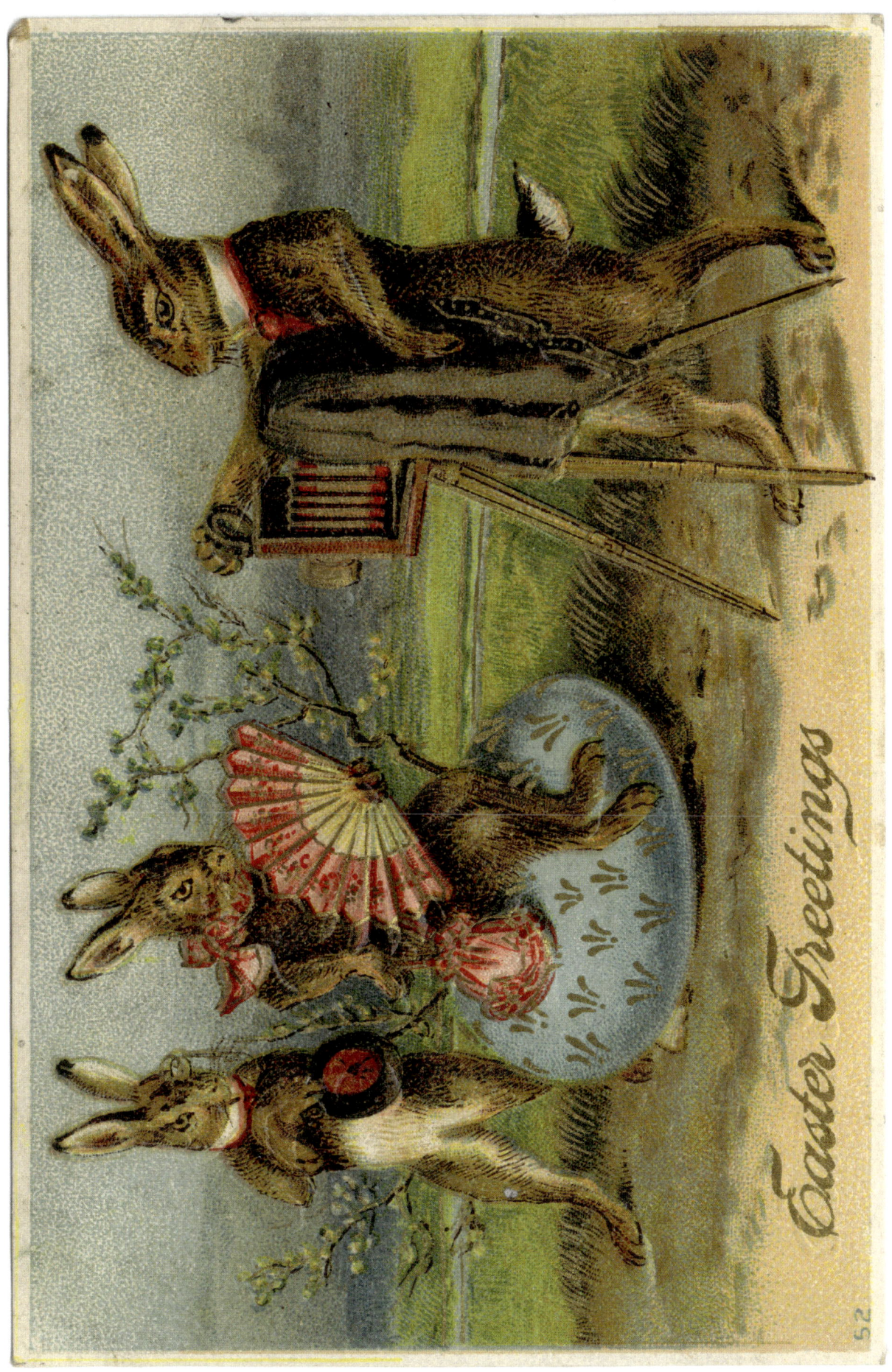

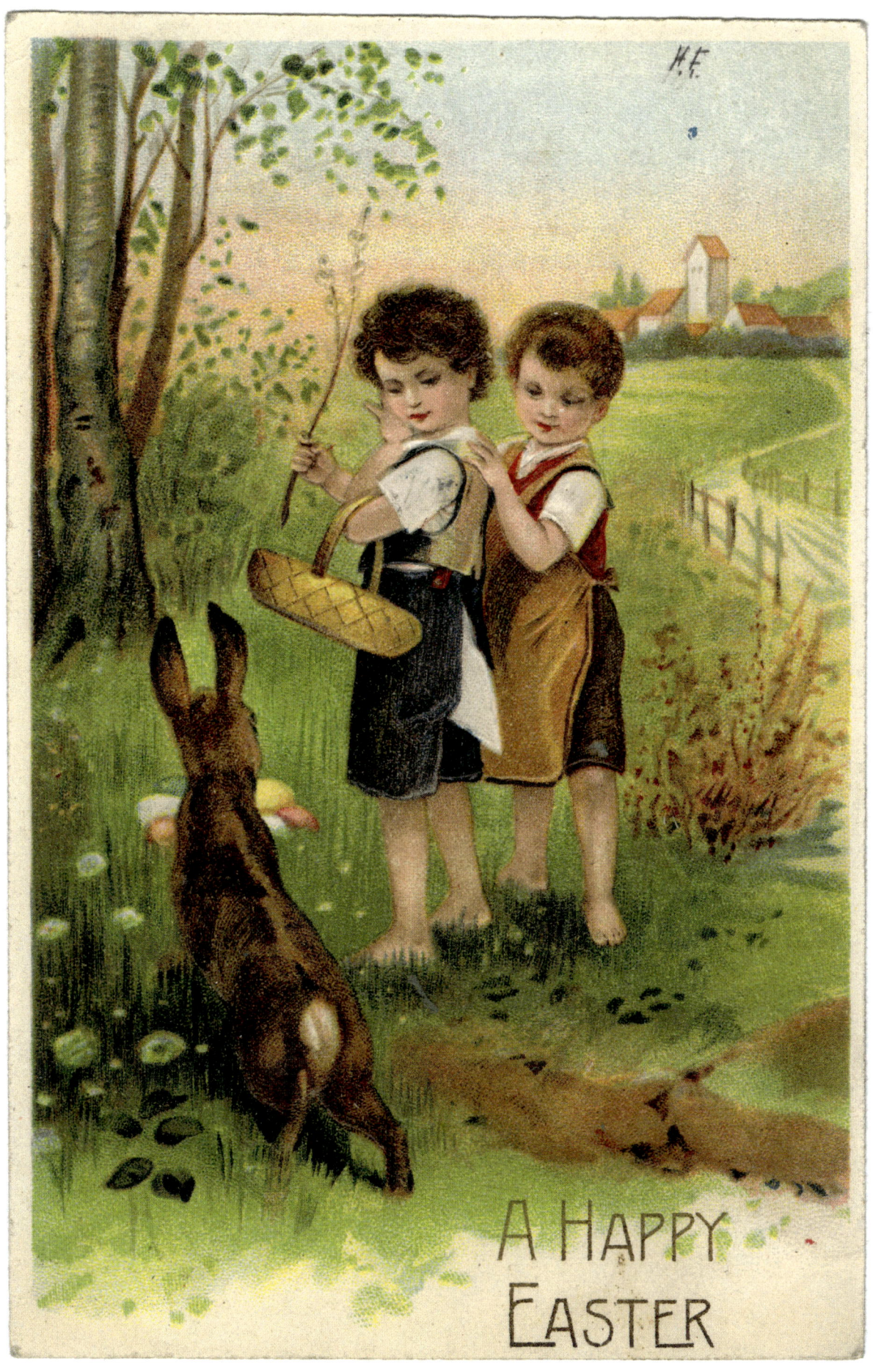

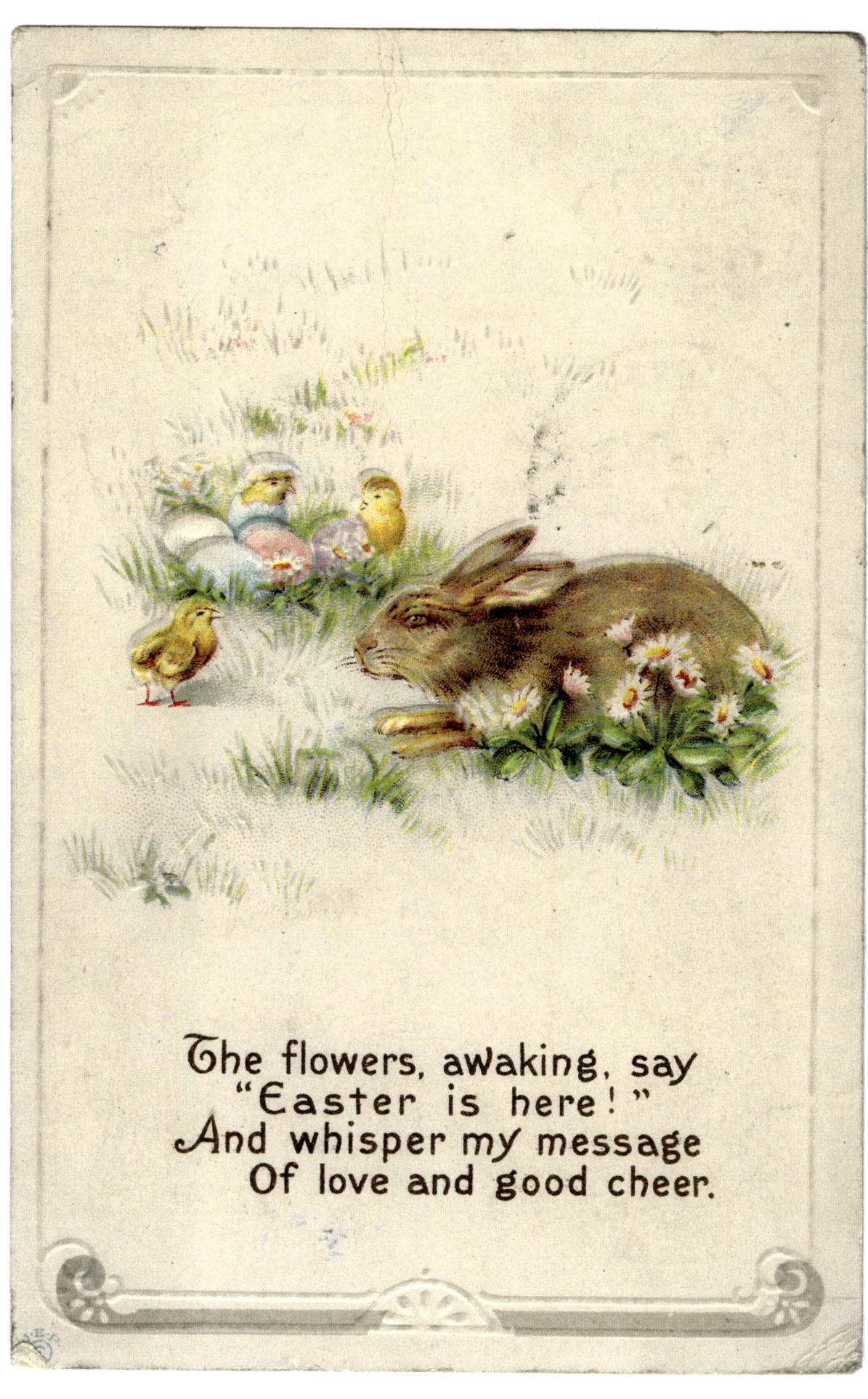

The flowers, awaking, say
"Easter is here!"
And whisper my message
Of love and good cheer.

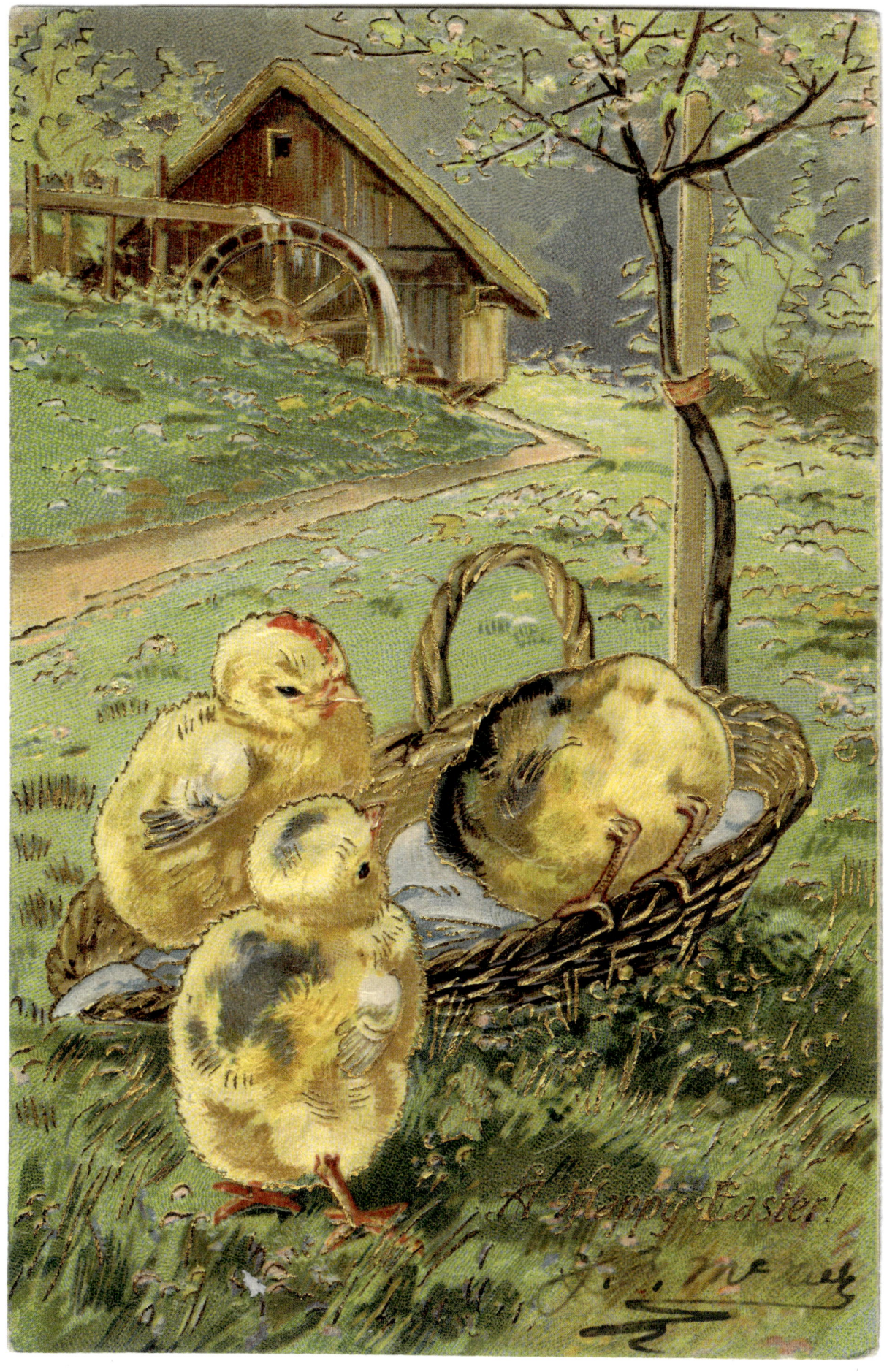

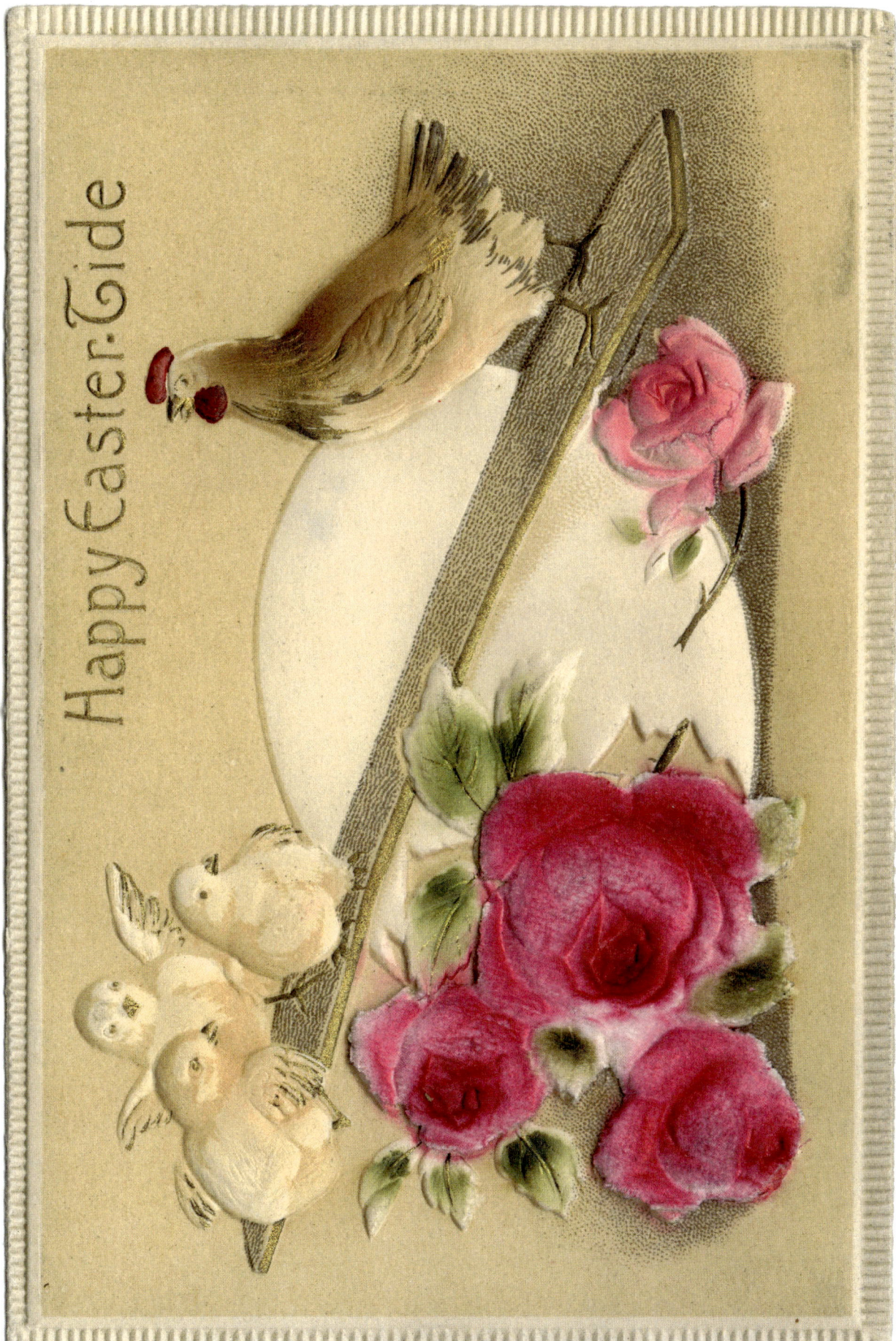

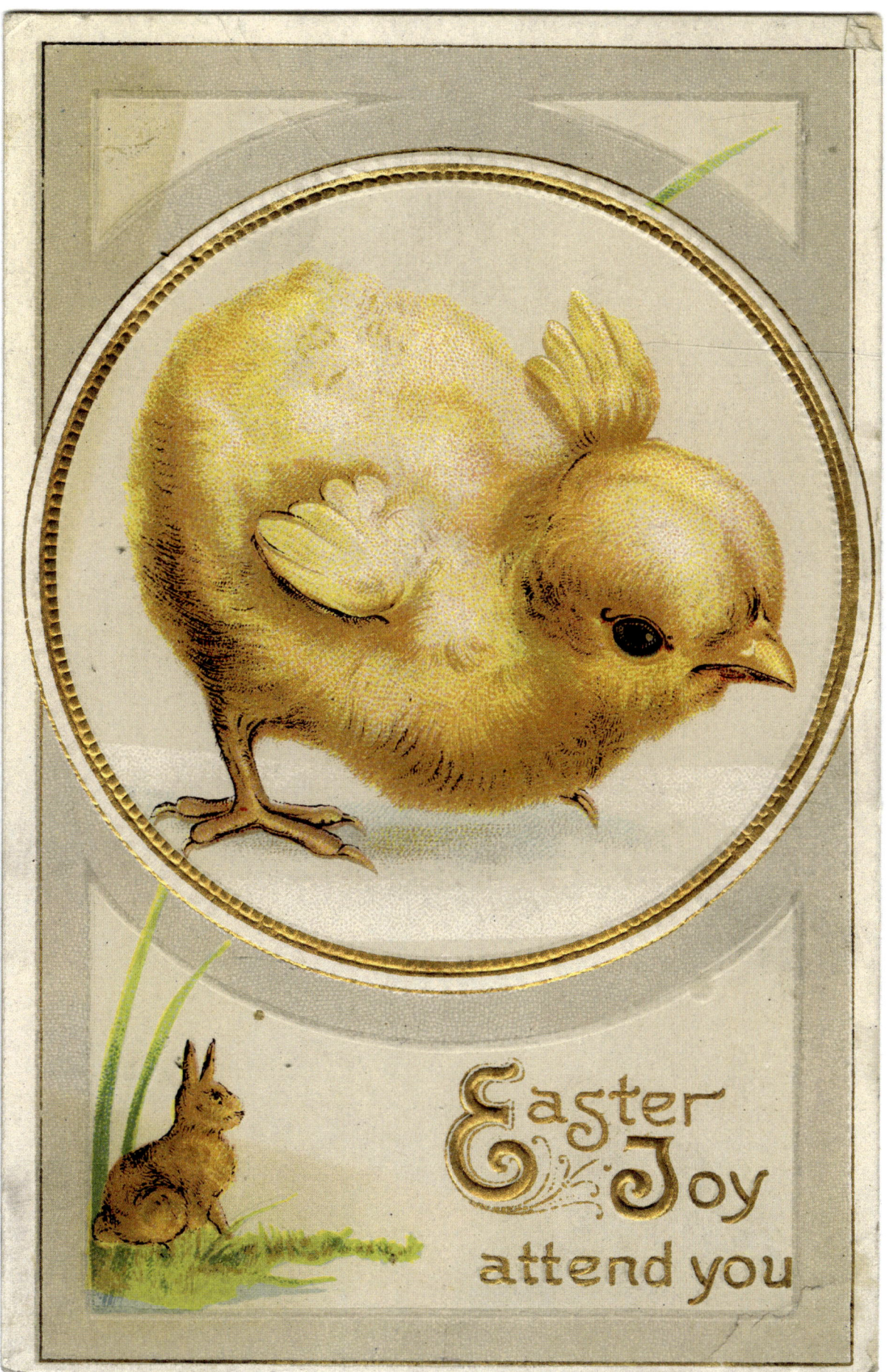

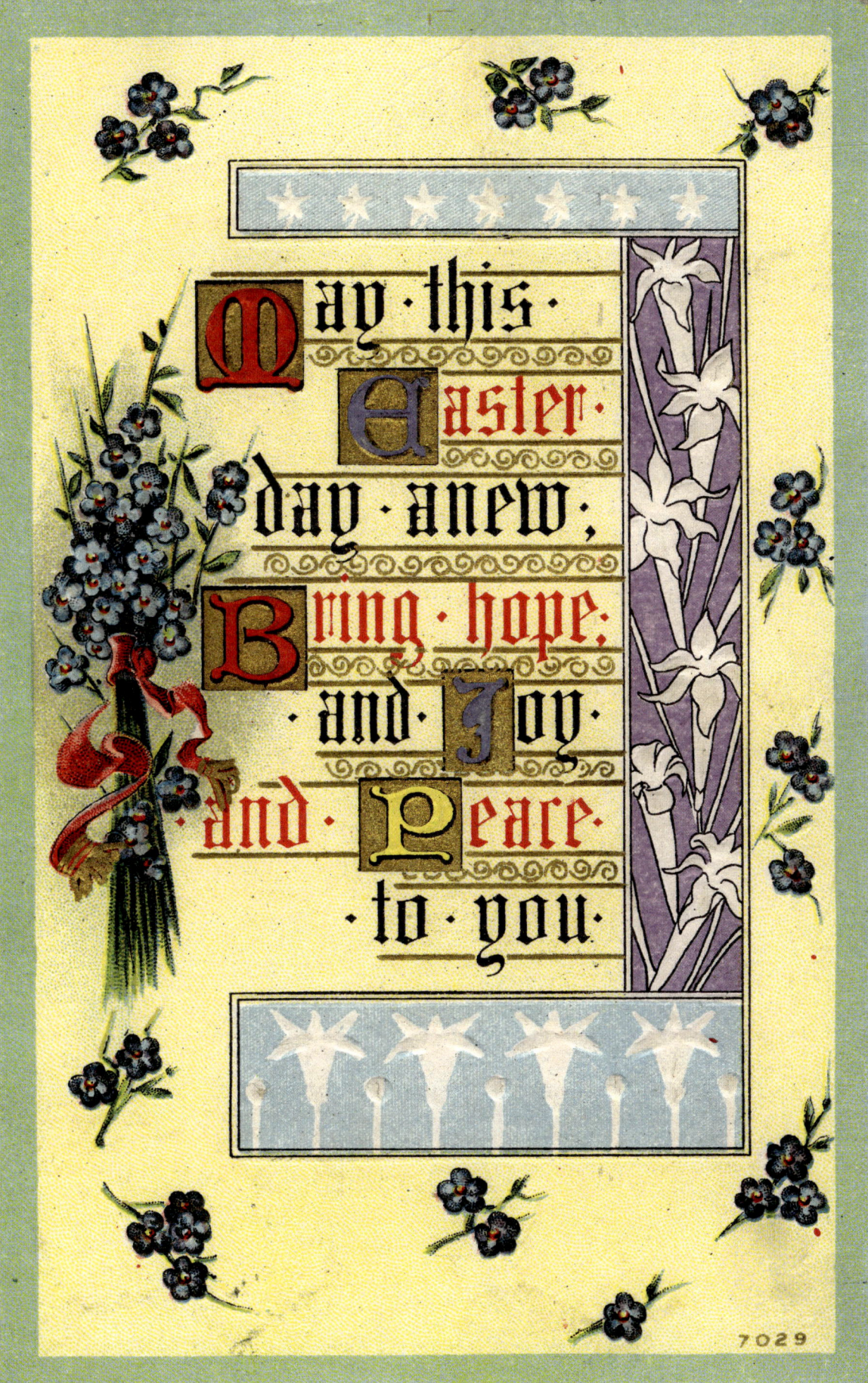

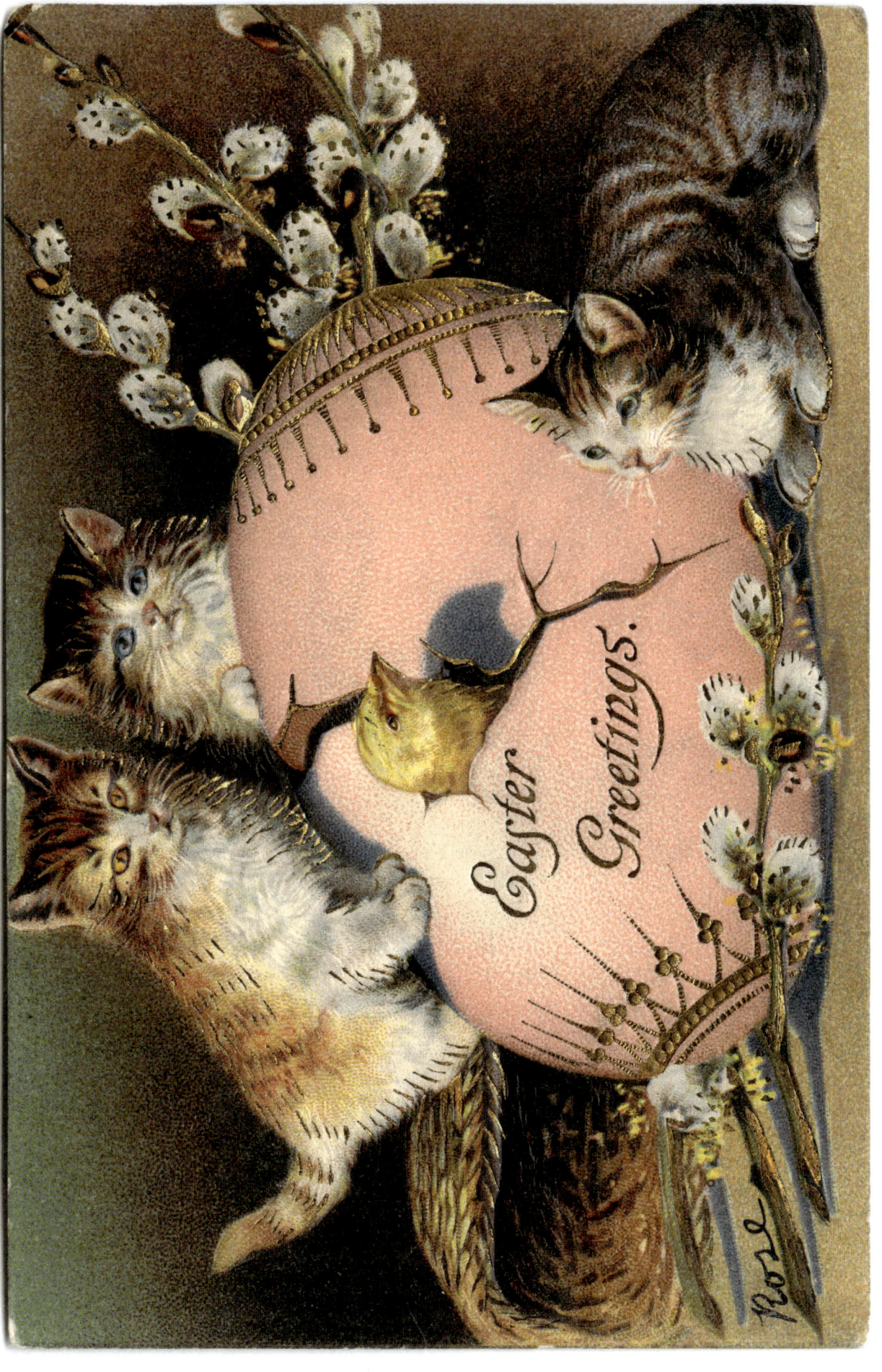

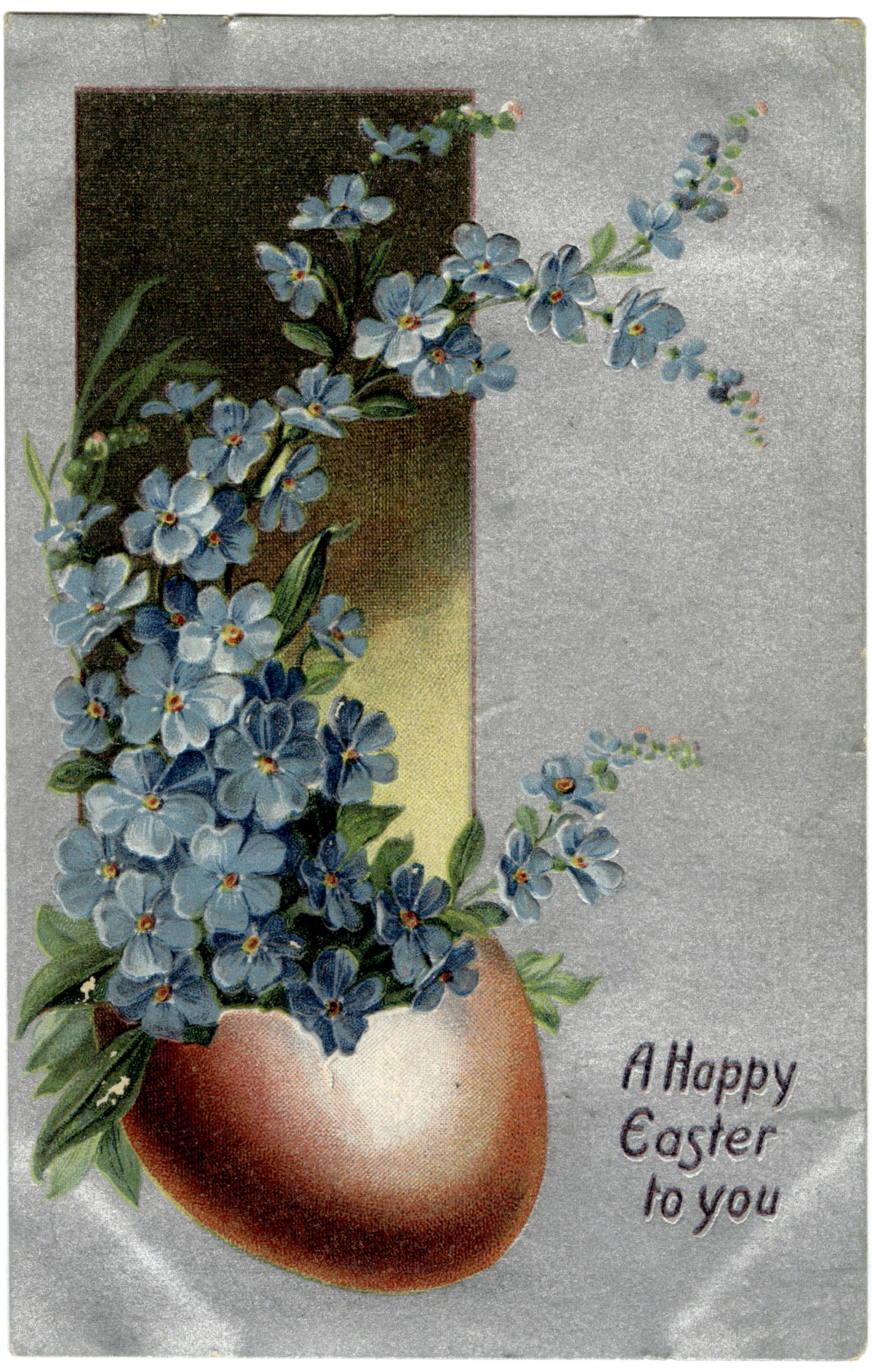

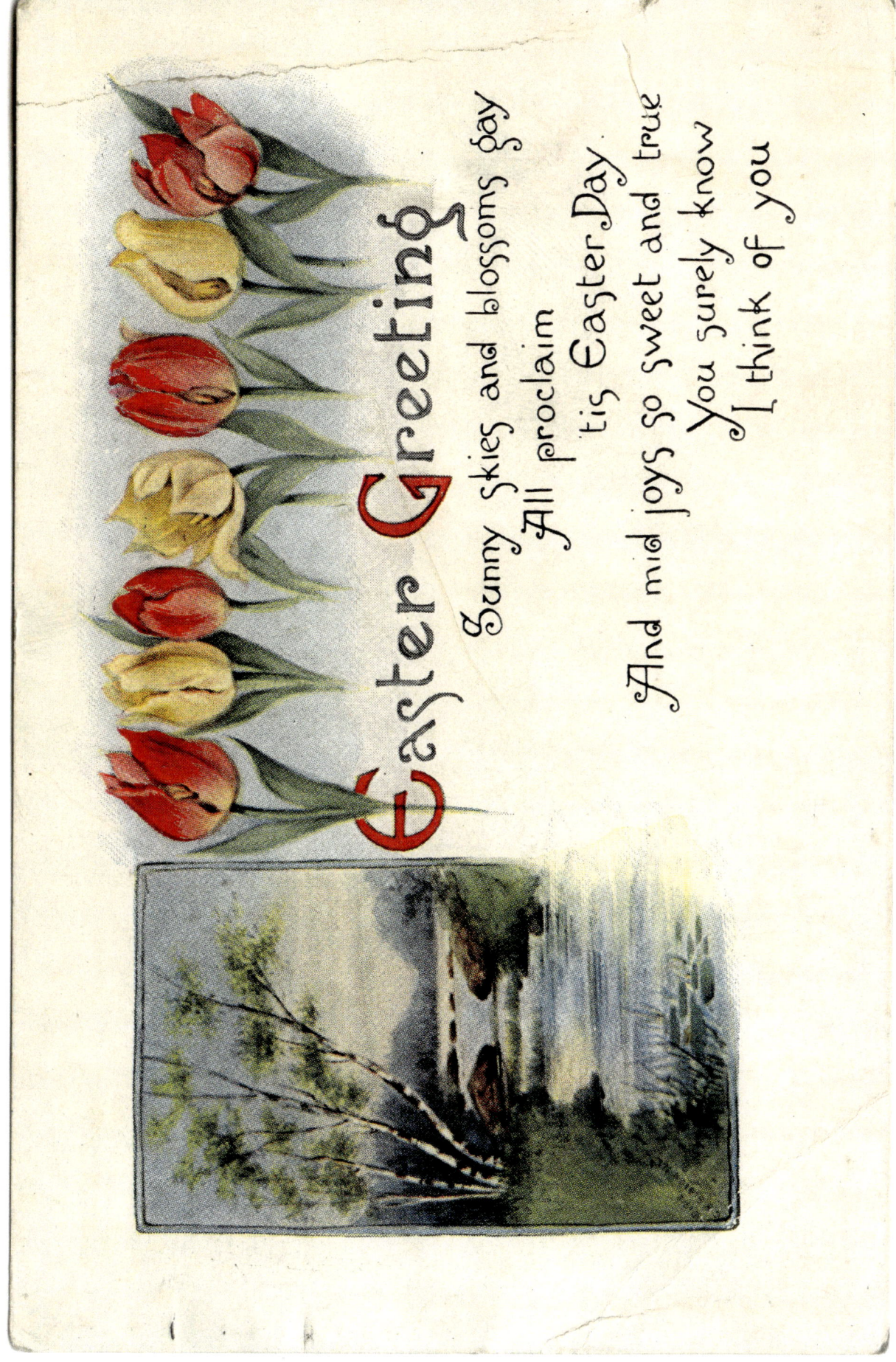

Easter Greeting

Sunny skies and blossoms gay
All proclaim 'tis Easter Day.
And mid joys so sweet and true
You surely know I think of you

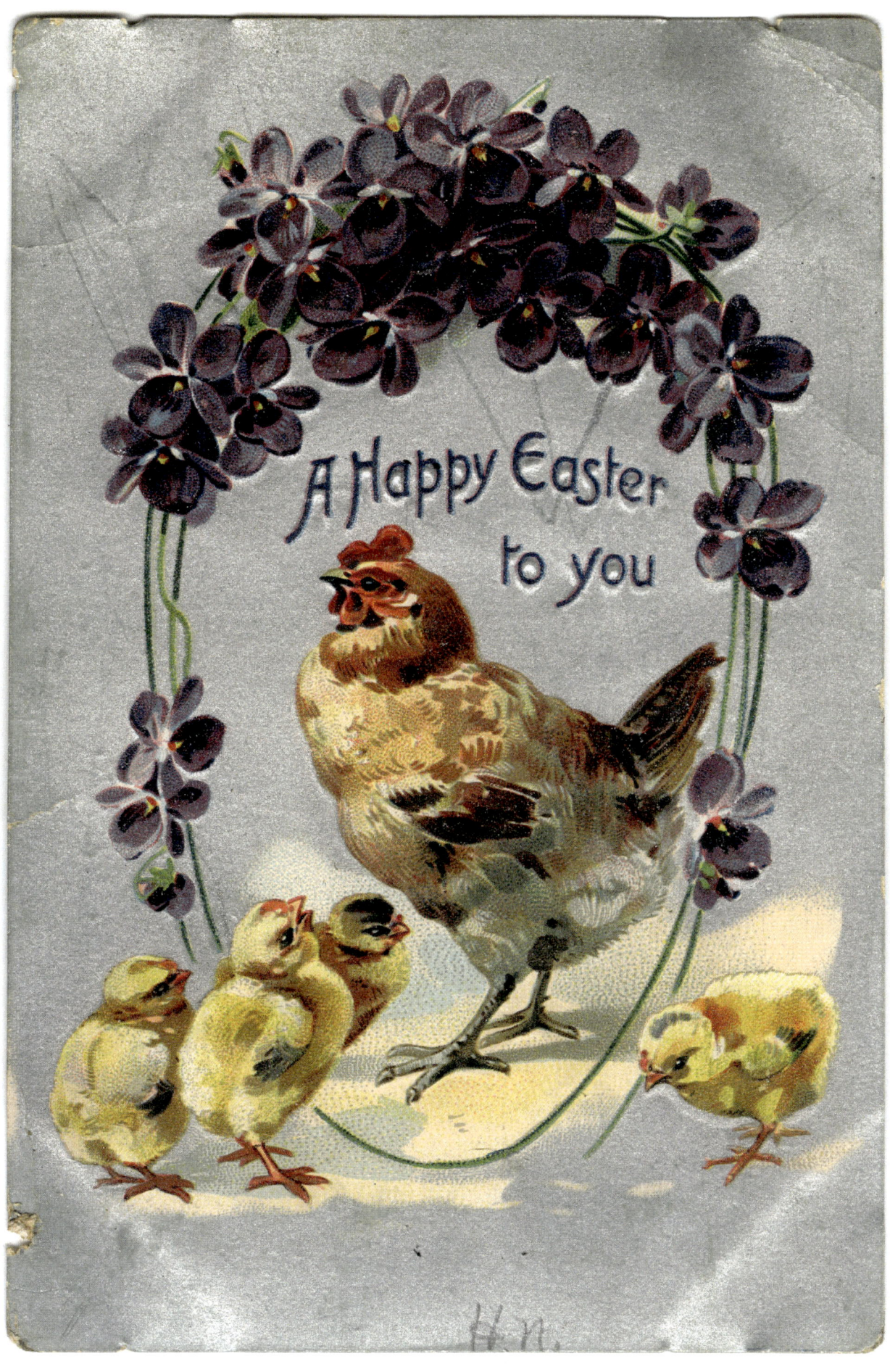

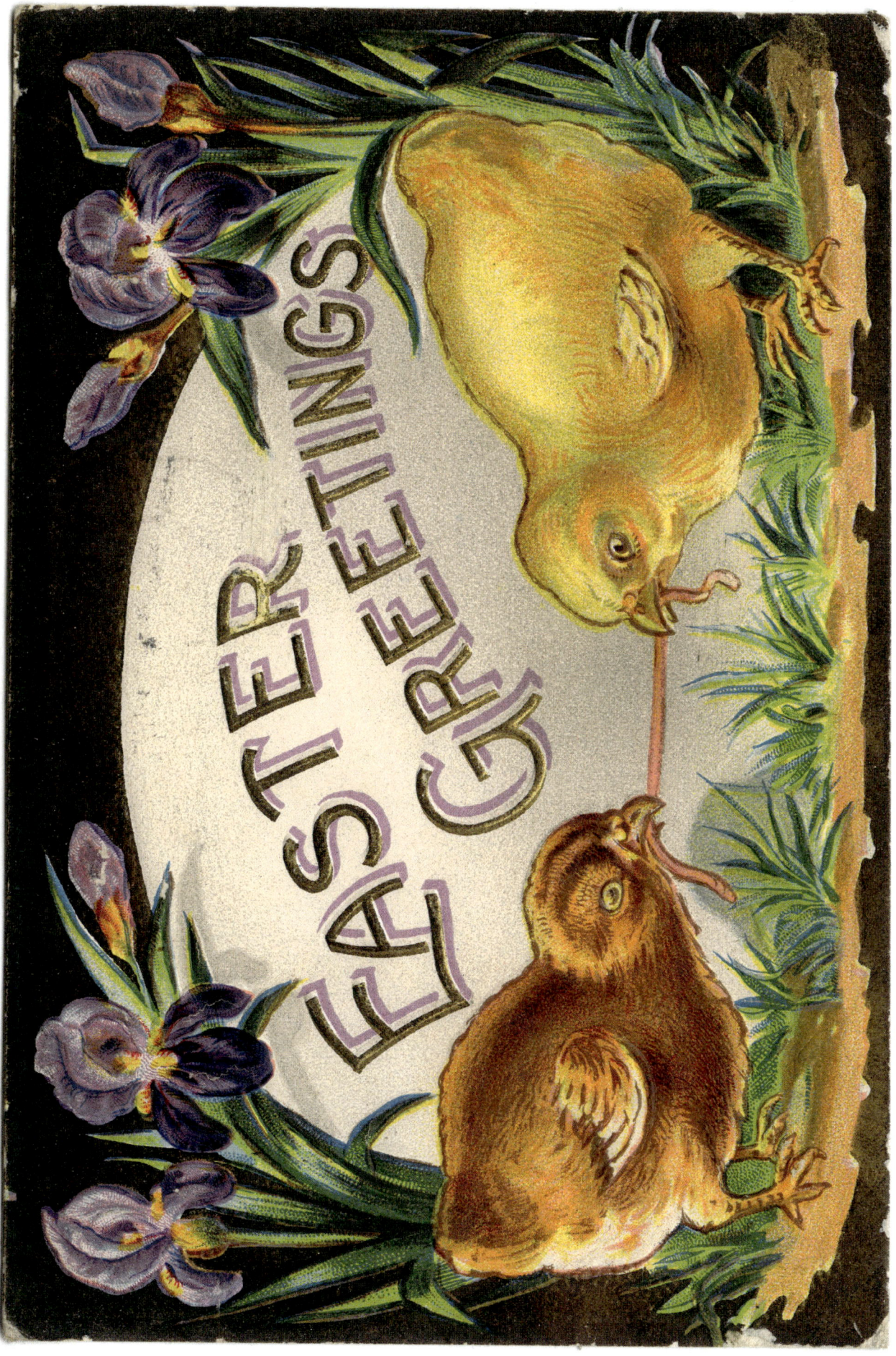

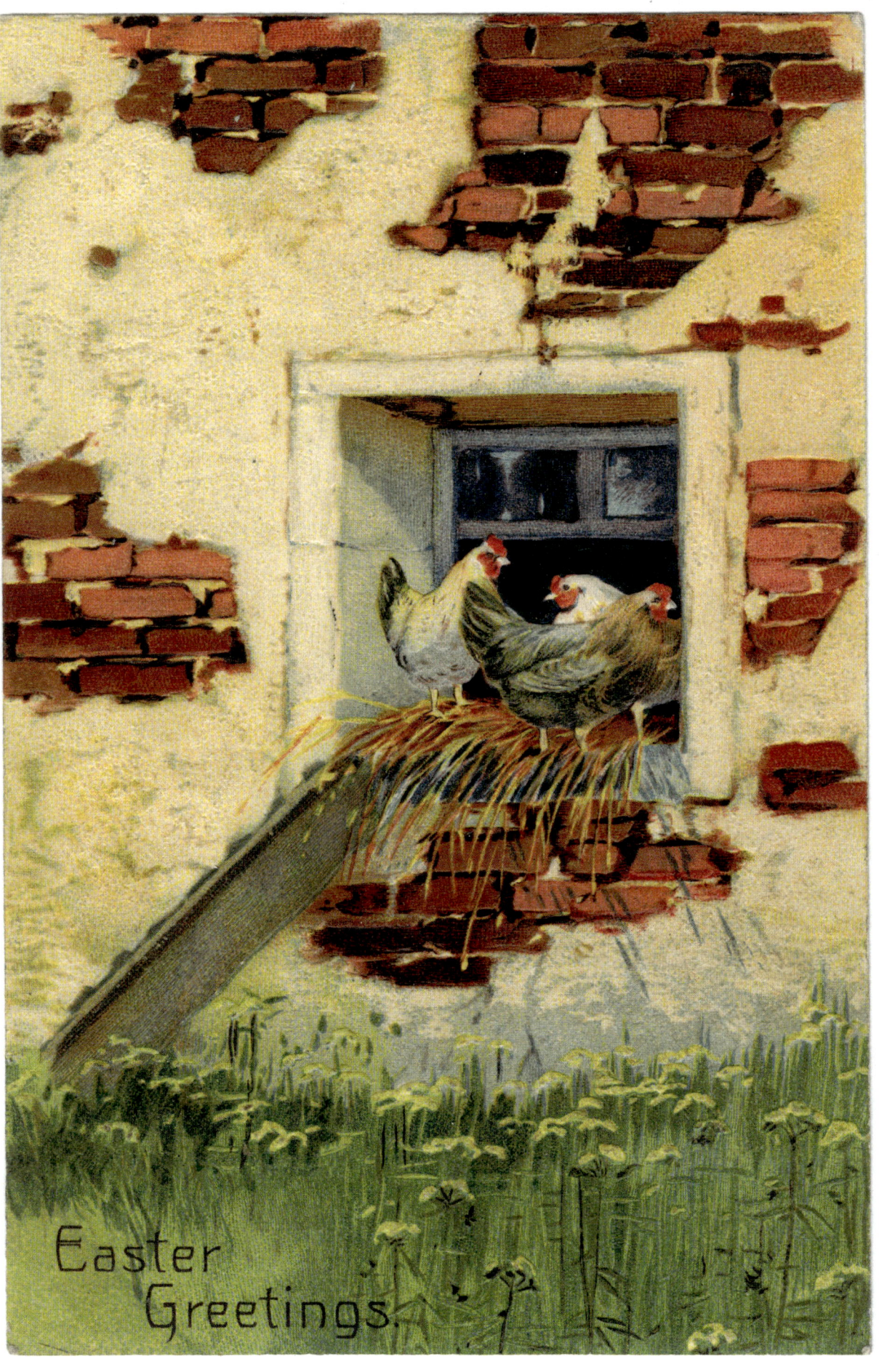

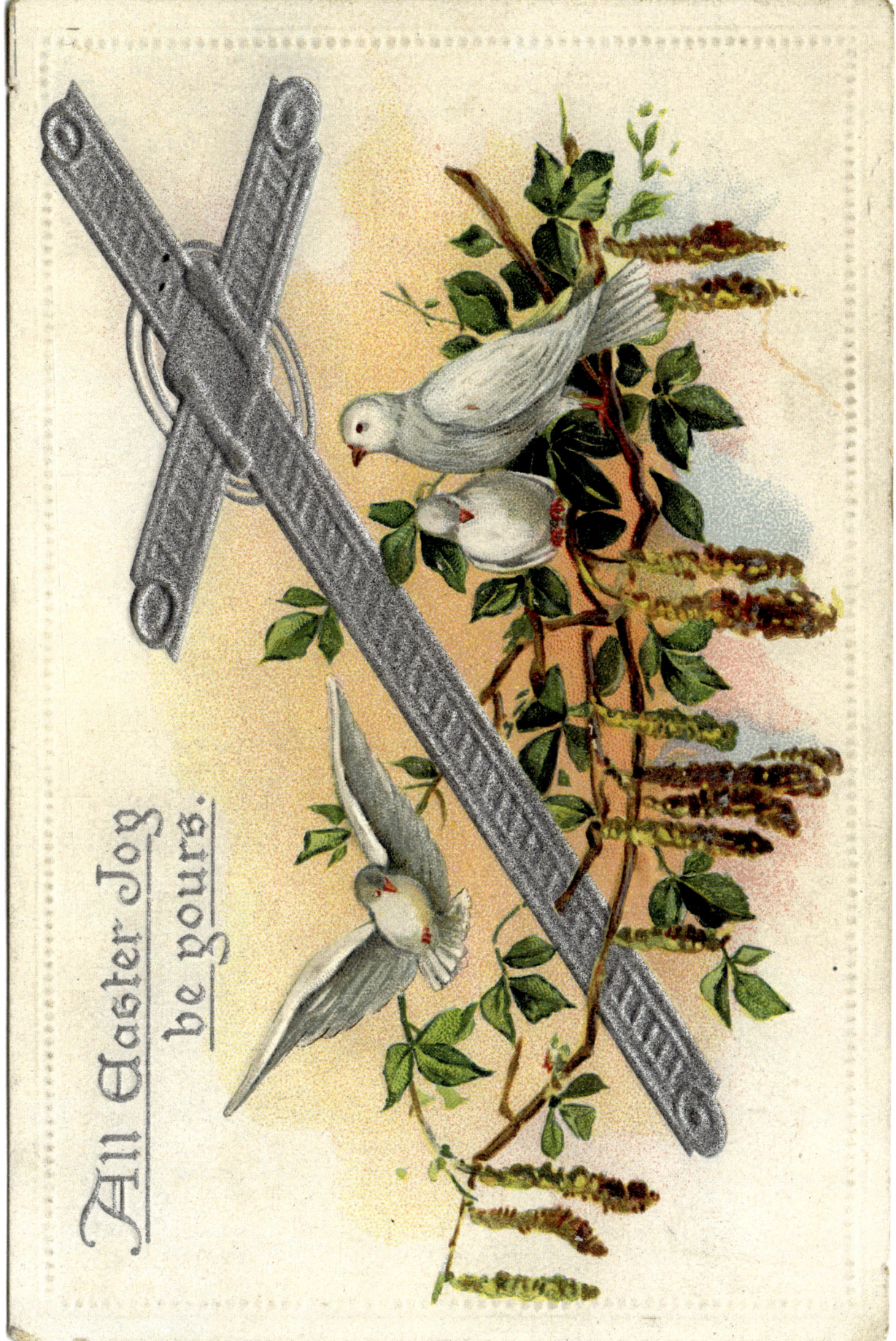
All Easter Joy be yours.

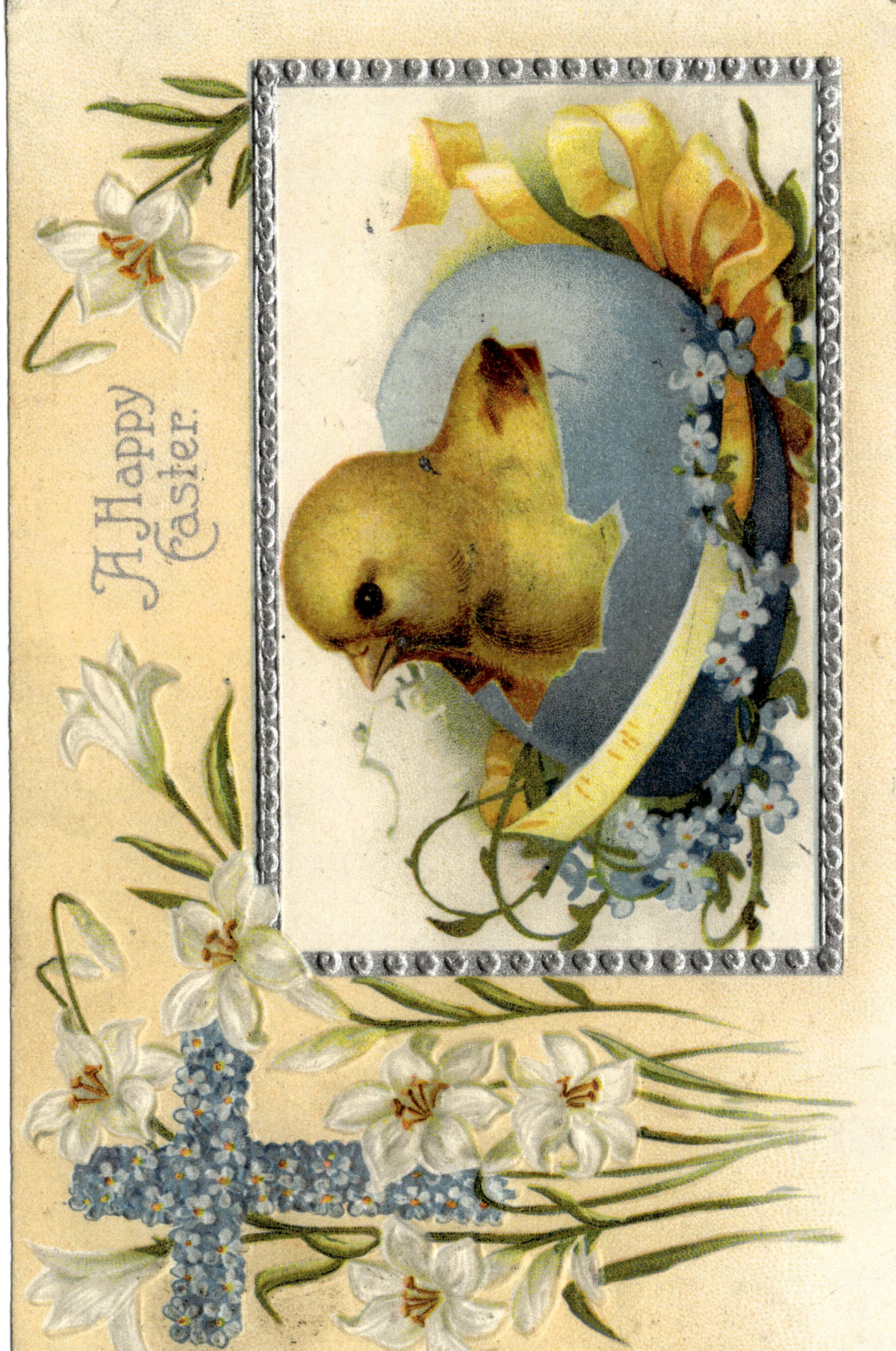

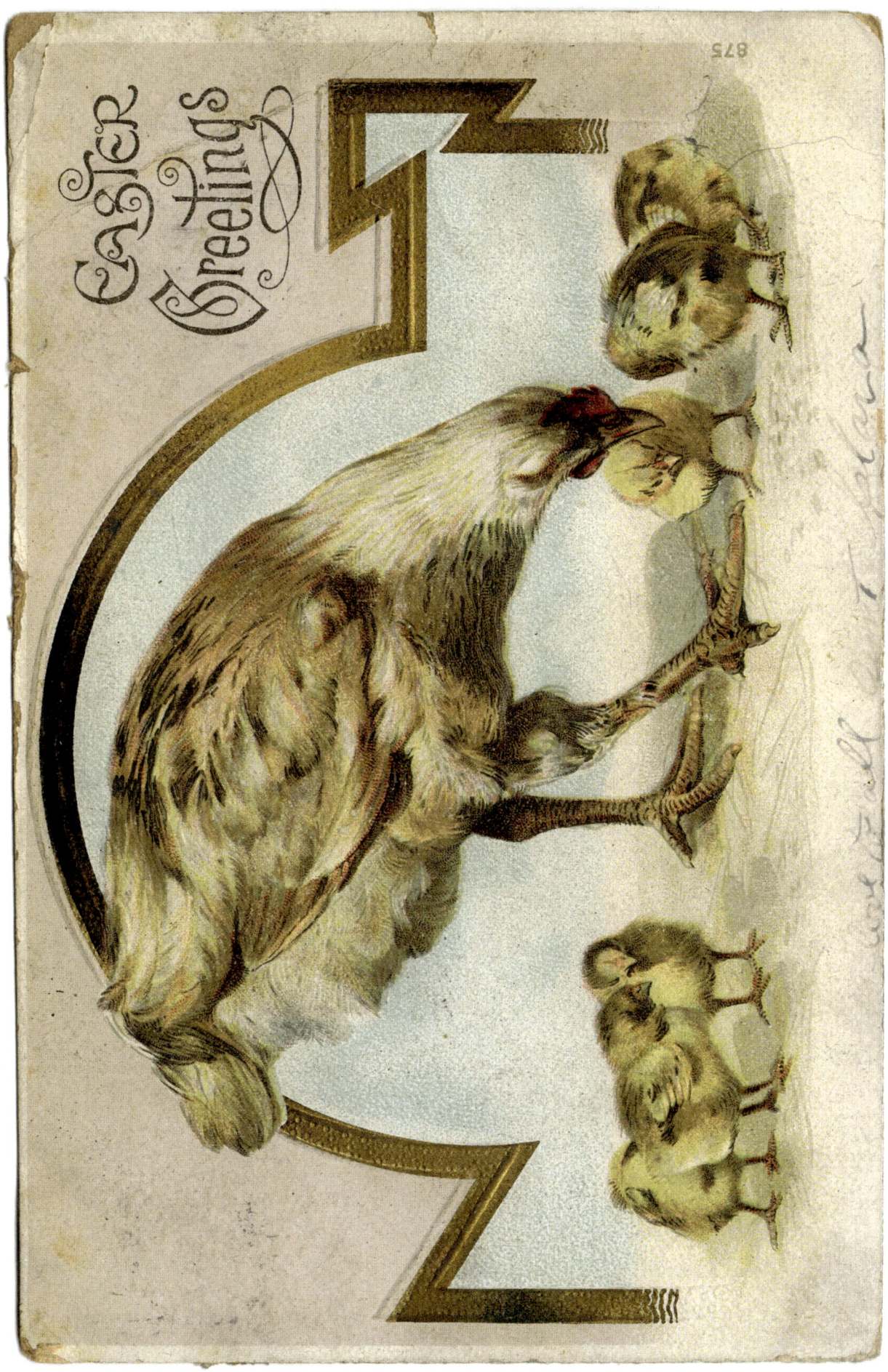

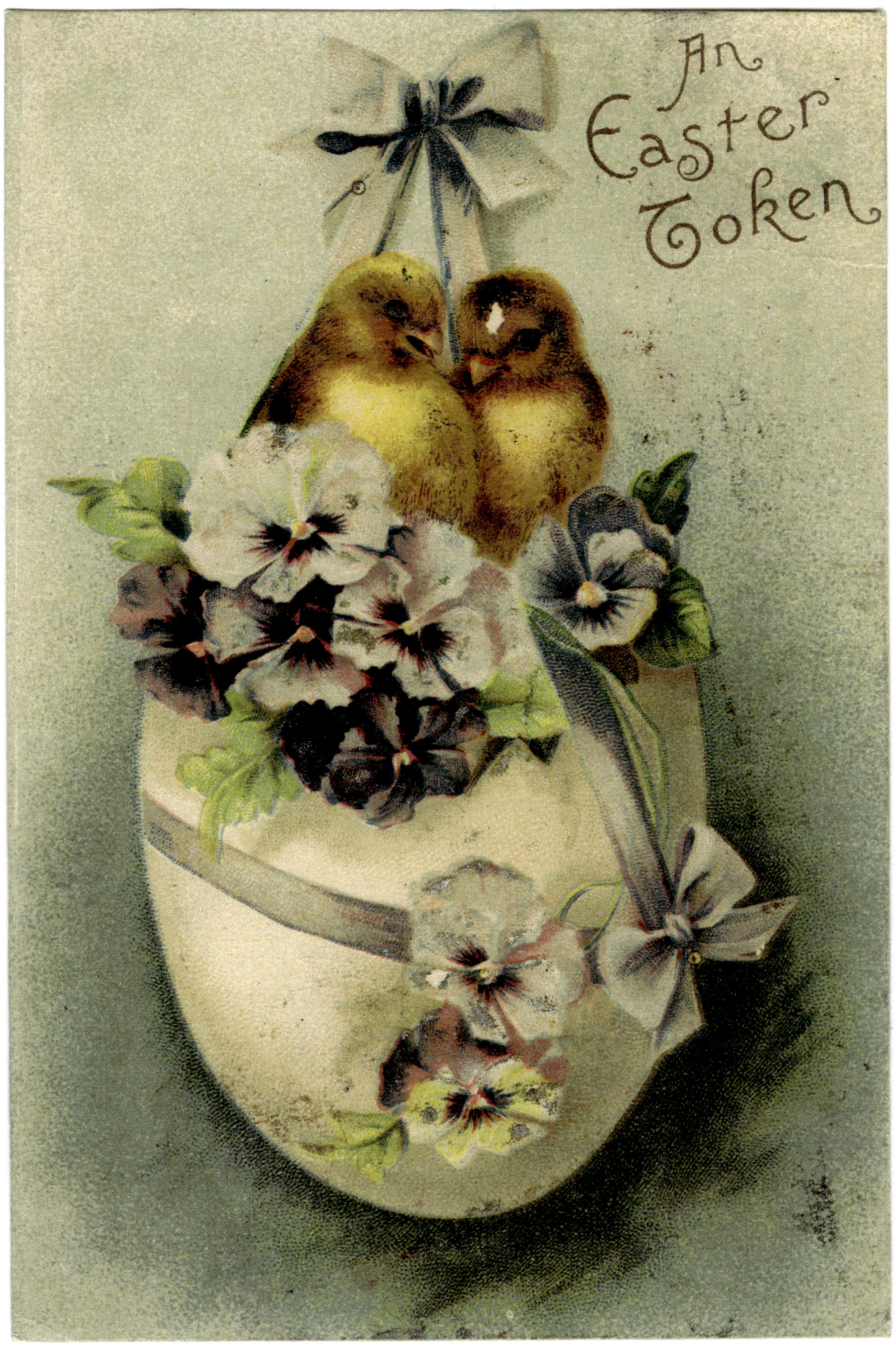

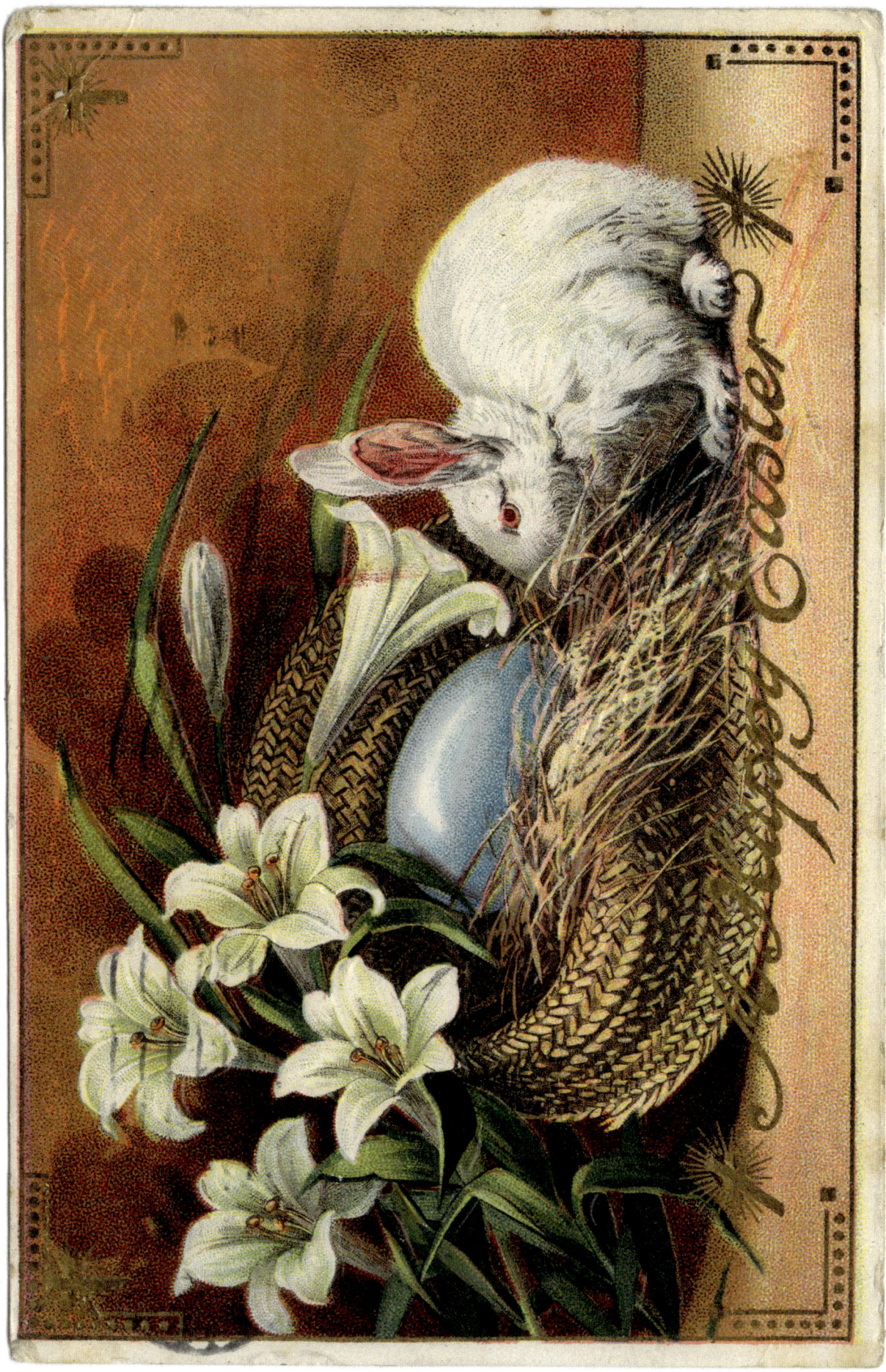

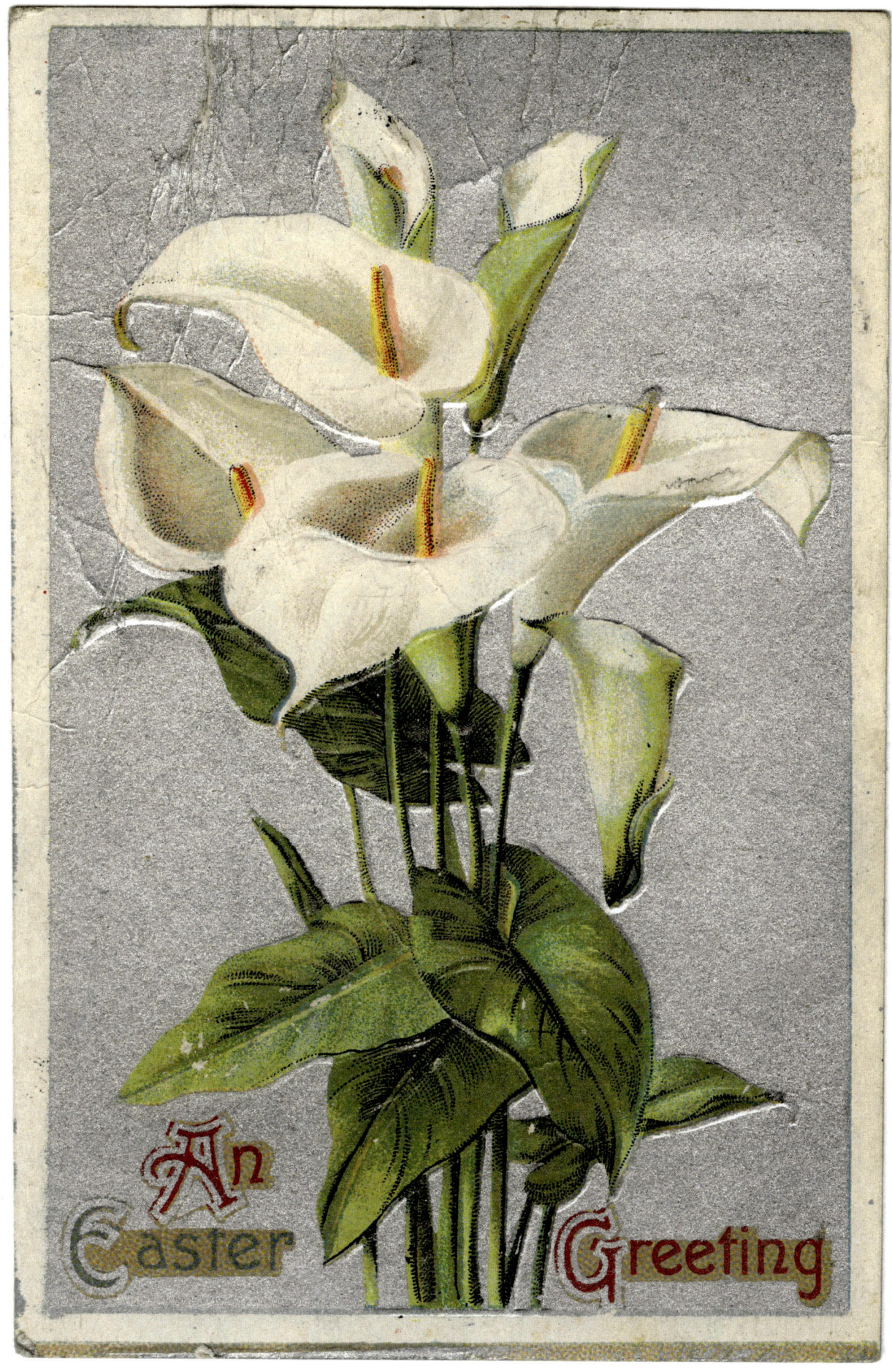

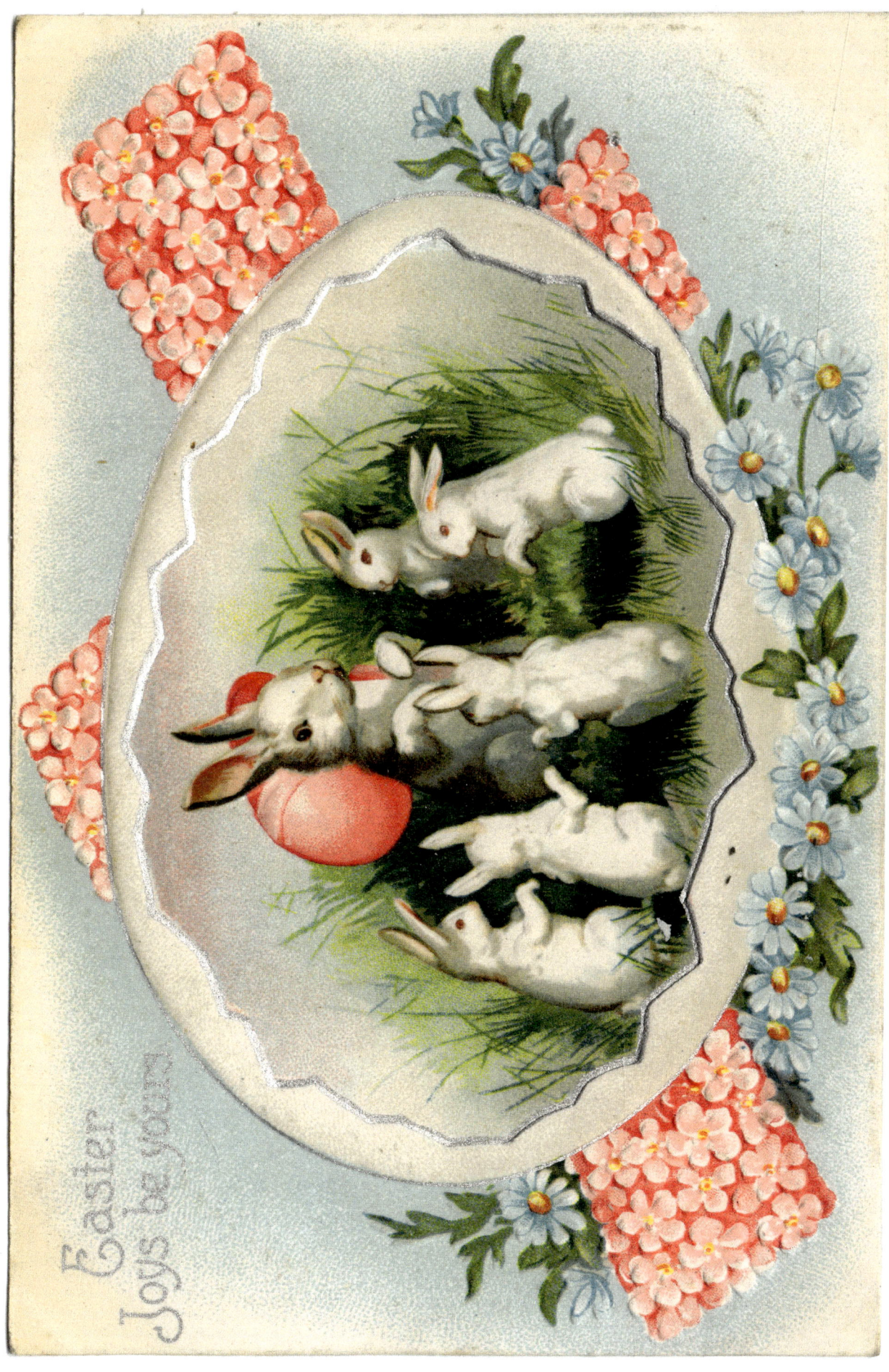

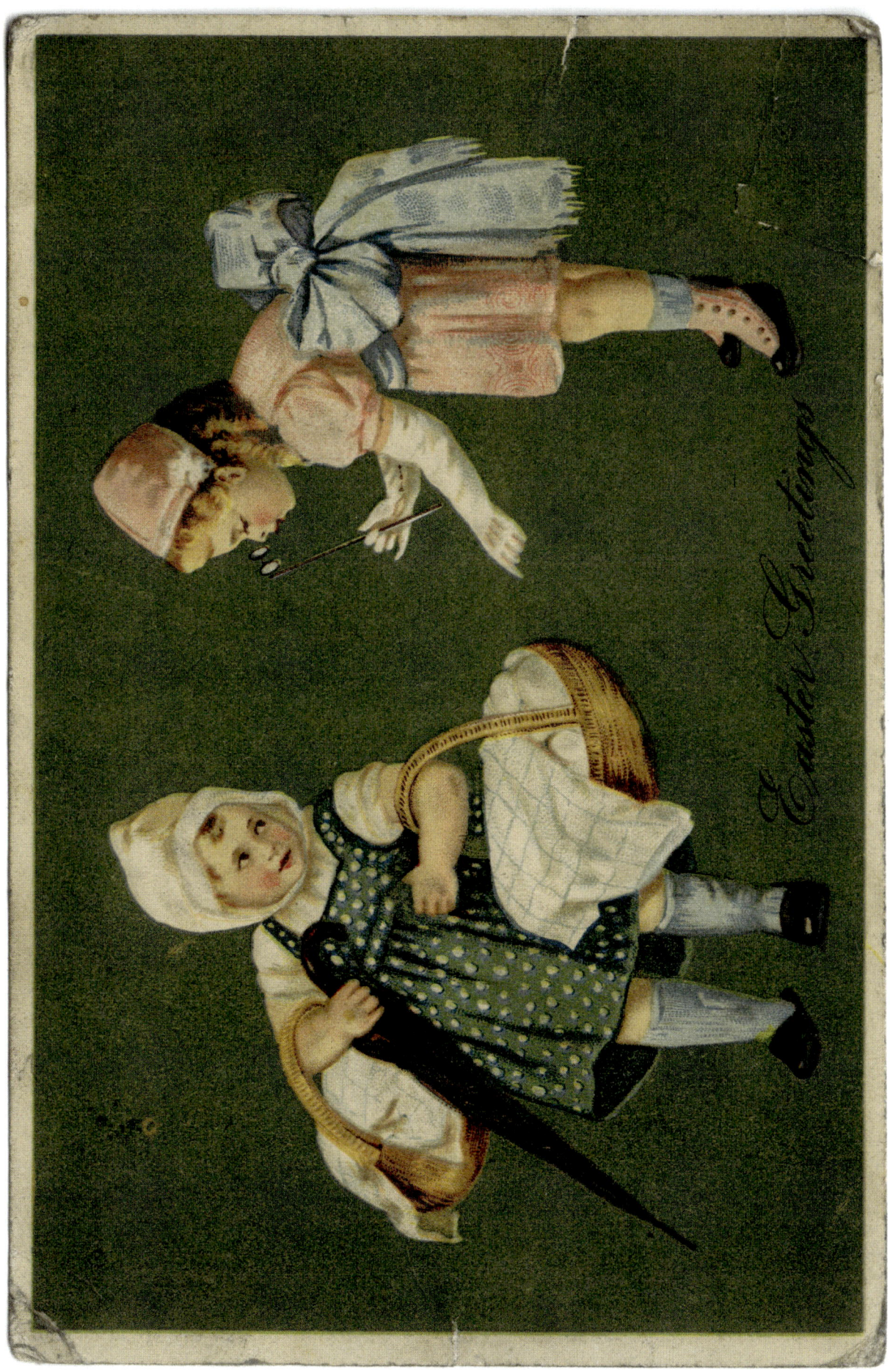
Easter Greetings

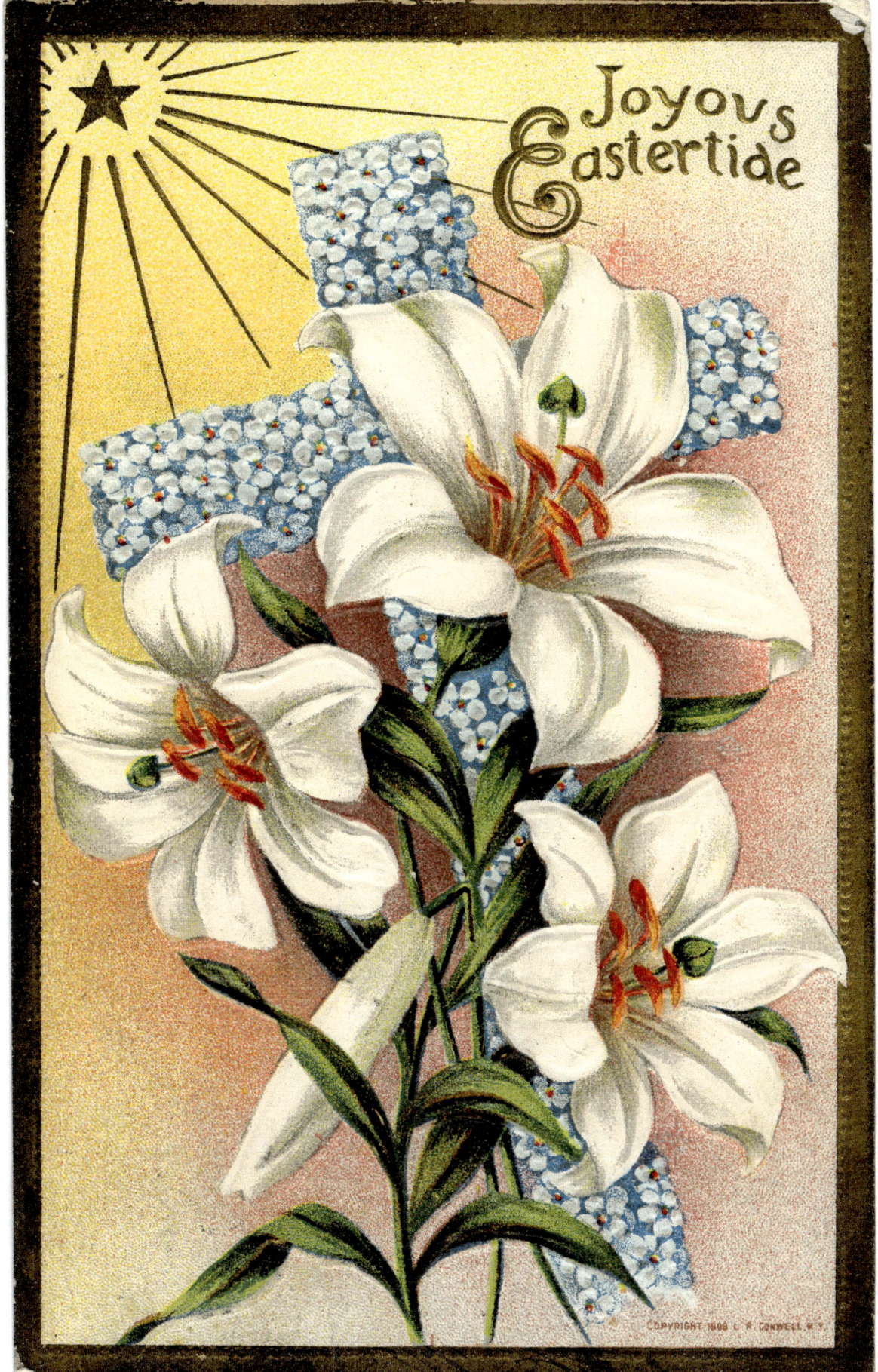

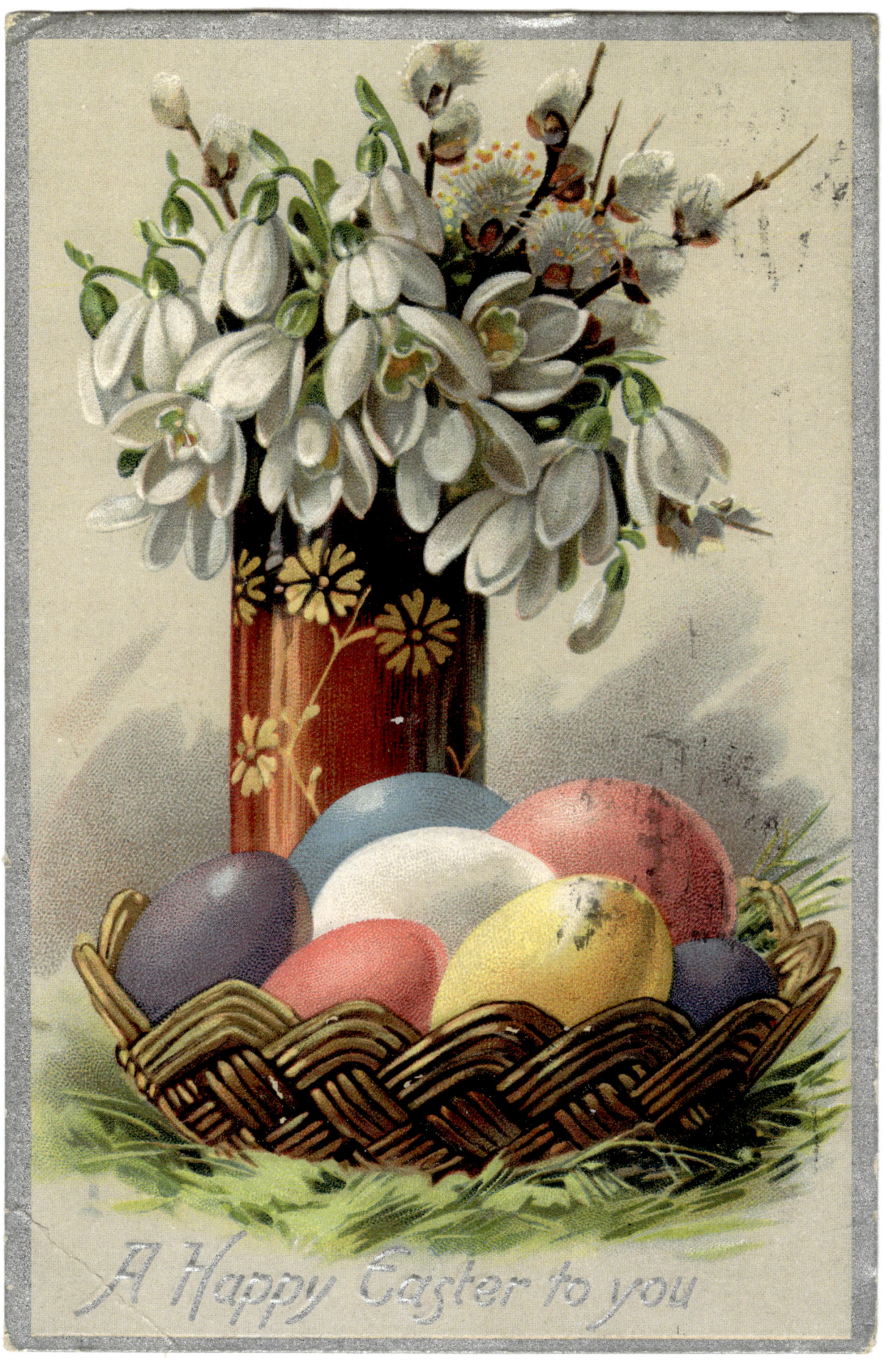

COMPLETE CATALOG OF BOOKS AT CGRPUBLISHING.COM

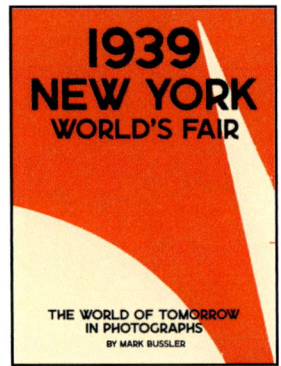
1939 New York World's Fair: The World of Tomorrow in Photographs

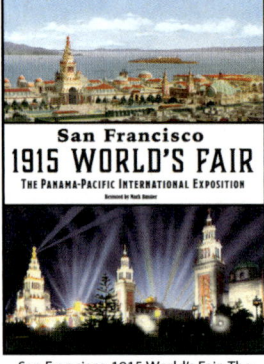
San Francisco 1915 World's Fair: The Panama-Pacific International Expo.

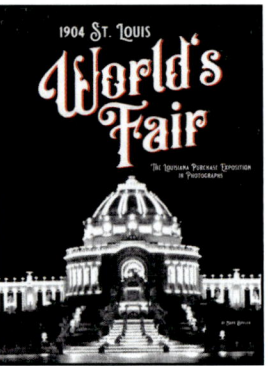
1904 St. Louis World's Fair: The Louisiana Purchase Exposition in Photographs

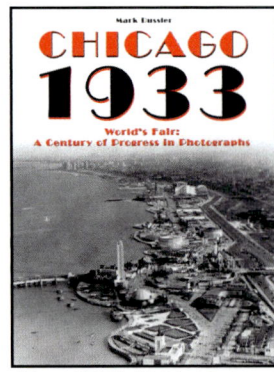
Chicago 1933 World's Fair: A Century of Progress in Photographs

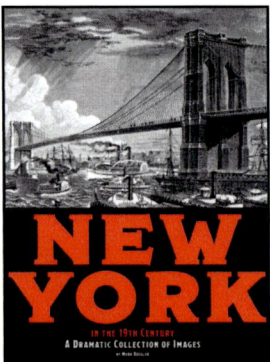
19th Century New York: A Dramatic Collection of Images

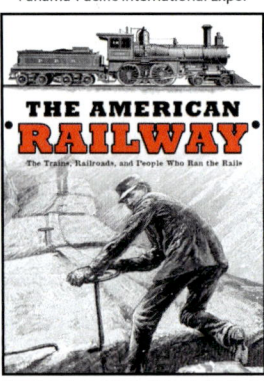
The American Railway: The Trains, Railroads, and People Who Ran the Rails

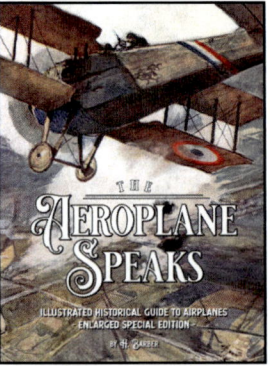
The Aeroplane Speaks: Illustrated Historical Guide to Airplanes

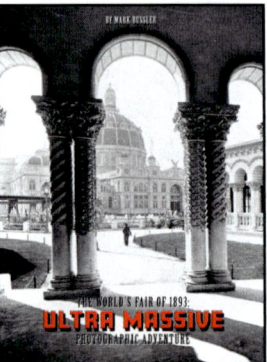
The World's Fair of 1893 Ultra Massive Photographic Adventure Vol. 1

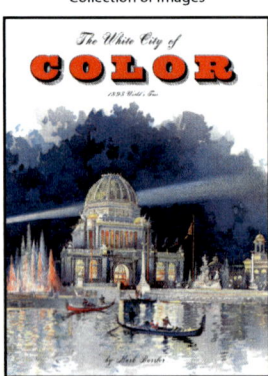
The White City of Color: 1893 World's Fair

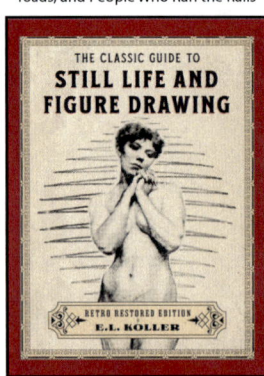
The Classic Guide to Still Life and Figure Drawing

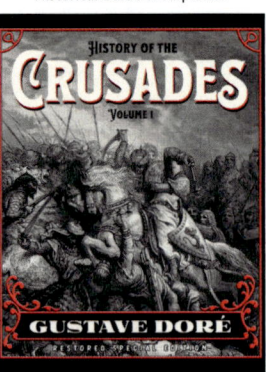
History of the Crusades: Gustave Doré Retro Restored Edition

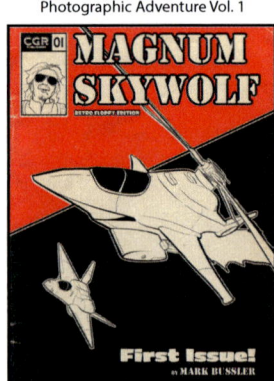
Magnum Skywolf #1

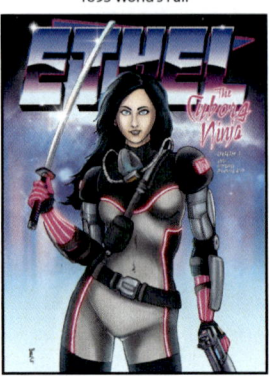
Ethel the Cyborg Ninja Book 1

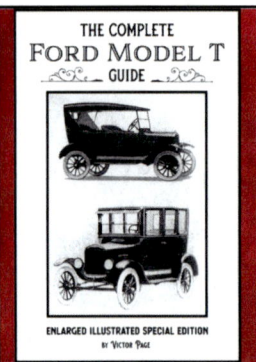
The Complete Ford Model T Guide: Enlarged Illustrated Special Edition

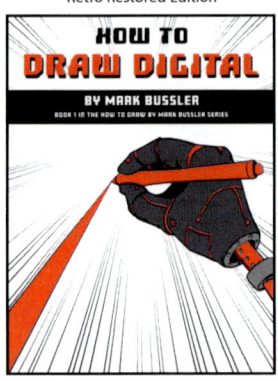
How To Draw Digital by Mark Bussler

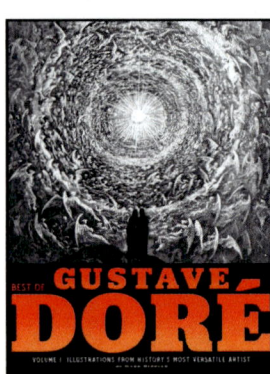
Best of Gustave Doré Volume 1: Illustrations from History's Most Versatile...

COMPLETE CATALOG OF BOOKS AT CGRPUBLISHING.COM

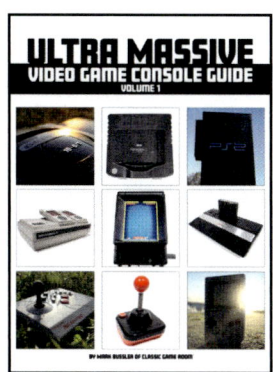
Ultra Massive Video Game Console Guide Volume 1

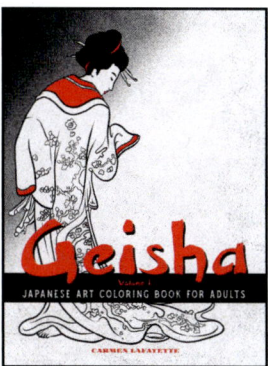
Geisha Japanese Art Coloring Book for Adults

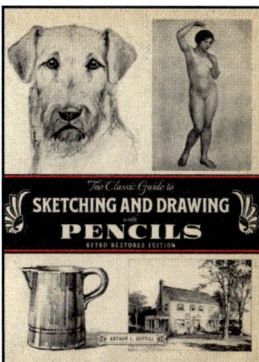
The Classic Guide to Sketching and Drawing with Pencils

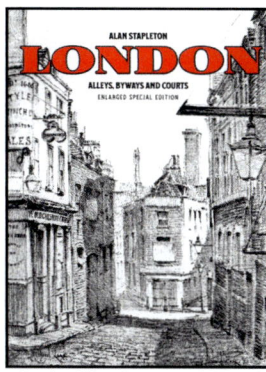
London Alleys, Byways, and Courts: Enlarged Special Edition

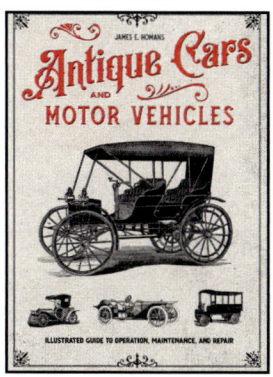
Antique Cars and Motor Vehicles: Illustrated Guide to Operation...

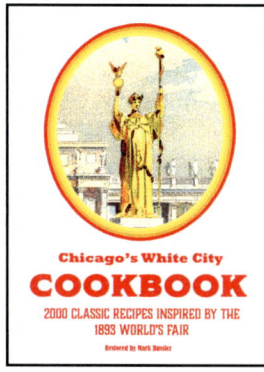
Chicago's White City Cookbook

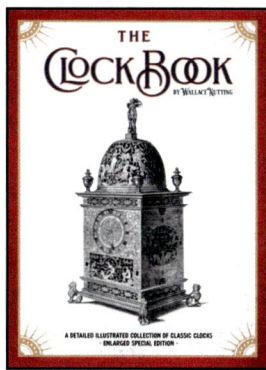
The Clock Book: A Detailed Illustrated Collection of Classic Clocks

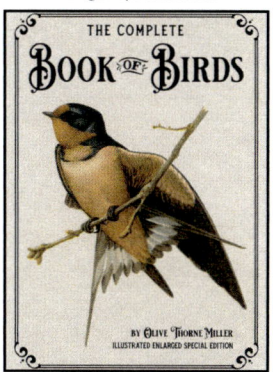
The Complete Book of Birds: Illustrated Enlarged Special Edition

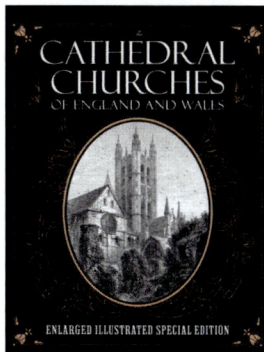
The Cathedral Churches of England and Wales: Enlarged Illustrated Special Ed.

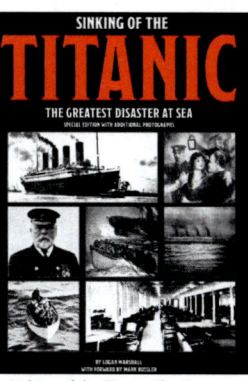
Sinking of the Titanic: The Greatest Disaster at Sea

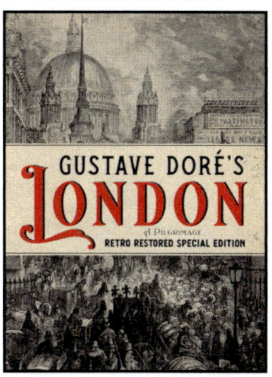
Gustave Doré's London: A Pilgrimage: Retro Restored Special Edition

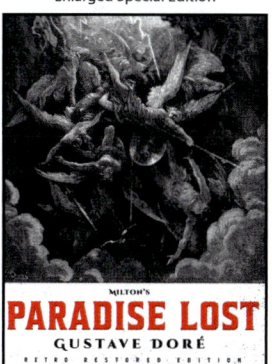
Milton's Paradise Lost: Gustave Doré Retro Restored Edition

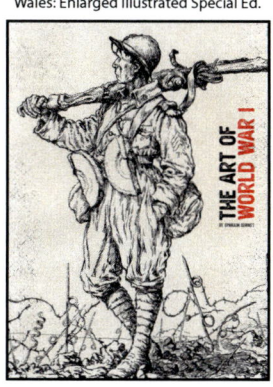
The Art of World War 1

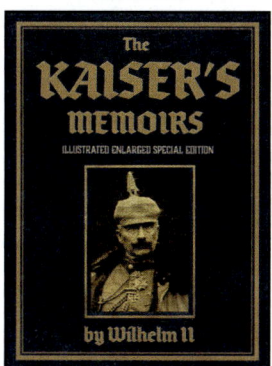
The Kaiser's Memoirs: Illustrated Enlarged Special Edition

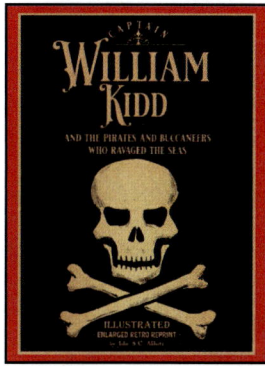
Captain William Kidd and the Pirates and Buccaneers Who Ravaged the Seas

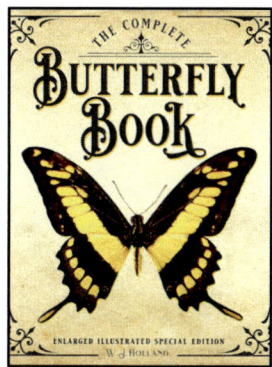
The Complete Butterfly Book: Enlarged Illustrated Special Edition

- MAILING LIST -
JOIN FOR EXCLUSIVE OFFERS

www.CGRpublishing.com/subscribe

Made in the USA
Monee, IL
13 March 2025